SIMON TAILSWORTH

THE AFRICAN FAT-TAILED GECKOS CARE

The complete guide to pet ownership

Copyright © 2025 by Simon Tailsworth

All rights reserved. No part of this publication may be reproduced, stored or transmitted in any form or by any means, electronic, mechanical, photocopying, recording, scanning, or otherwise without written permission from the publisher. It is illegal to copy this book, post it to a website, or distribute it by any other means without permission.

Simon Tailsworth asserts the moral right to be identified as the author of this work.

Simon Tailsworth has no responsibility for the persistence or accuracy of URLs for external or third-party Internet Websites referred to in this publication and does not guarantee that any content on such Websites is, or will remain, accurate or appropriate.

Designations used by companies to distinguish their products are often claimed as trademarks. All brand names and product names used in this book and on its cover are trade names, service marks, trademarks and registered trademarks of their respective owners. The publishers and the book are not associated with any product or vendor mentioned in this book. None of the companies referenced within the book have endorsed the book.

First edition

*This book was professionally typeset on Reedsy.
Find out more at reedsy.com*

Contents

1	Chapter 1: Introduction to African Fat-Tailed Geckos	1
2	Chapter 2: Understanding Reptile Biology	5
3	Chapter 3: Preparing for Your Gecko	9
4	Chapter 4: Setting Up the Ideal Habitat	13
5	Chapter 5: Feeding and Nutrition Essentials	17
6	Chapter 6: Understanding Behavior and Handling	21
7	Chapter 7: Health Monitoring and Common Illnesses	25
8	Chapter 8: Shedding, Growth, and Molting Care	29
9	Chapter 9: Breeding Basics and Genetics	33
10	Chapter 10: Advanced Feeding and Dietary Enrichment	37
11	Chapter 11: Creating a Long-Term Care Plan	41
12	Chapter 12: Problem-Solving and Troubleshooting	45
13	Chapter 13: Enrichment, Exercise, and Mental Stimulation	49
14	Chapter 14: Ethical Considerations and Community Engagement	53
15	Chapter 15: Lifelong Learning and Conservation Awareness	57

One

Chapter 1: Introduction to African Fat-Tailed Geckos

African fat-tailed geckos (Hemitheconyx caudicinctus) are a captivating and increasingly popular species in the reptile pet trade, known for their distinctive appearance, manageable size, and gentle temperament. Native to West Africa, these geckos offer both beginners and experienced reptile enthusiasts an accessible yet rewarding experience in pet keeping. Understanding their natural history, characteristics, and care needs is essential before welcoming one into a home environment.

Overview of the Species: Origin, Habitat, and Natural Behavior

African fat-tailed geckos originate primarily from the savannah and semi-arid regions of West Africa, including countries such as Ghana, Togo, and Nigeria. In their natural habitat, they experience distinct wet and dry seasons, which influence their activity patterns and reproductive cycles. Unlike tropical rainforest species, fat-tailed geckos thrive in environments with moderate humidity, dry substrates, and a range of hiding spots among rocks and sparse vegetation.

In the wild, these geckos are primarily nocturnal. They spend most of the day hidden under rocks, within crevices, or burrowed into loose soil to avoid predators and extreme temperatures. At night, they emerge to hunt insects and other small invertebrates, displaying patient and deliberate hunting techniques. This nocturnal behavior is mirrored in captivity, where they often become more active during the evening hours. Observing these natural behaviors is both fascinating and instructive for gecko keepers, as it guides decisions regarding enclosure design, feeding schedules, and enrichment.

African fat-tailed geckos are also adept at camouflage, utilizing their muted coloration to blend seamlessly into their surroundings. In addition to their defensive coloration, they rely on their tails as a survival tool. In moments of threat, the tail can serve as a distraction; in some cases, they may even voluntarily drop their tail to escape predators, a process known as autotomy. The tail will eventually regenerate, although the new tail may differ in appearance from the original.

Key Characteristics: Size, Coloration, Lifespan, and Temperament

One of the defining features of African fat-tailed geckos is their stout, muscular tail, which is typically nearly as wide as the body. This tail not only serves as a fat storage organ, providing energy during periods of scarcity, but also contributes to their signature silhouette. Adult fat-tailed geckos typically range from six to nine inches in total length, with females usually slightly smaller than males.

Coloration in this species varies from pale beige or sandy tones to darker browns and grays, often accompanied by bands or spots along the body and tail. Selective breeding in captivity has produced a variety of morphs, including albino, high yellow, and patternless variants. Despite the diversity of morphs, all retain the species' characteristic thick tail and gentle facial features.

Lifespan is another appealing trait for prospective keepers. African fat-tailed geckos are relatively long-lived, often reaching 15 to 20 years in captivity with proper care. Some individuals have been documented living beyond 20 years, making them a long-term commitment for dedicated pet owners.

Temperament is perhaps the most inviting aspect of this species. African fat-tailed geckos are generally docile, tolerant of handling, and show minimal stress responses when managed properly. Unlike some gecko species that are highly skittish or aggressive, fat-tailed geckos often display curiosity toward human interaction, making them suitable for both display and educational purposes.

Differences Between African Fat-Tailed Geckos and Other Gecko Species

While African fat-tailed geckos share some characteristics with other popular gecko species, they possess several distinct differences that influence their care requirements. Unlike leopard geckos (Eublepharis macularius), which are also popular in captivity, fat-tailed geckos tend to be slightly more robust in body shape and have a proportionally thicker tail. Their coloration patterns are generally more muted than the bold spots and bands of leopard geckos, which can make them appear more naturalistic in display terrariums.

Unlike arboreal geckos, such as crested geckos (Correlophus ciliatus) or tokay geckos (Gekko gecko), African fat-tailed geckos are strictly terrestrial. They spend the majority of their time on the ground rather than climbing, which affects the type of enclosure setup required. A horizontally oriented tank with adequate substrate for burrowing is more appropriate than a vertical setup, which is essential for arboreal species.

Furthermore, their nocturnal habits differentiate them from day-active geckos, influencing feeding times and lighting requirements. While some geckos require specialized UVB lighting for health, African fat-tailed geckos are crepuscular and do not have the same strict UVB needs, although low-level UVB can still be beneficial. These differences underscore the importance of species-specific care and prevent keepers from applying general gecko husbandry principles indiscriminately.

Appeal and Suitability as Pets: Who They Are Best For

African fat-tailed geckos are ideal for a broad spectrum of reptile enthusiasts, from complete beginners to experienced keepers seeking a manageable, long-lived species. Their small size, docile nature, and relatively low-maintenance requirements make them particularly suitable for first-time gecko owners. A basic enclosure setup with a few hides, appropriate substrate, and a consistent feeding schedule is sufficient to maintain a healthy, content gecko.

For more experienced keepers, fat-tailed geckos offer opportunities for advanced husbandry, selective breeding, and morph exploration. The variety of available morphs allows for collection-focused enthusiasts to explore genetics, while breeding can be both a rewarding and educational experience when done ethically.

Additionally, their nocturnal behavior and manageable size make them excellent pets for individuals with limited space or those who enjoy observing subtle animal behaviors. They are also suitable for households with older children or adults, provided that handling is gentle and consistent to maintain trust and minimize stress.

In conclusion, African fat-tailed geckos present a unique combination of charm, adaptability, and manageable care requirements that make them an excellent choice for anyone interested in reptile pet keeping. By understanding their origin, natural behavior, key characteristics, and differences from other gecko species, prospective owners are better equipped to provide an enriching and responsible environment. Whether for beginners seeking a low-stress introduction to gecko care or experienced keepers exploring advanced breeding and husbandry, the African fat-tailed gecko offers a rewarding and long-term companionship. Their longevity, gentle temperament, and captivating appearance ensure that these geckos remain a beloved species in the reptile-keeping community.

Two

Chapter 2: Understanding Reptile Biology

A thorough understanding of reptile biology is essential for providing proper care to African fat-tailed geckos. Unlike mammals or birds, reptiles have unique physiological and behavioral adaptations that influence their health, feeding, and environmental needs. By learning the basics of anatomy, growth, shedding, and metabolism, owners can create a habitat that supports long-term well-being while recognizing signs of potential health issues early.

Basic Anatomy and Physiology Relevant to Care

African fat-tailed geckos, like all reptiles, are ectothermic, meaning their body temperature is regulated primarily by the external environment rather than internal metabolic processes. This characteristic has major implications for their care, as proper temperature gradients within the enclosure are critical to digestion, activity, and overall health.

Physically, fat-tailed geckos have a stout, muscular body with a distinctive fat-storing tail, which serves as a critical energy reserve during periods of food scarcity or stress. Their limbs are relatively short but strong, adapted for terrestrial movement and burrowing, rather than climbing. The skin of these geckos is covered in small, granular scales that offer protection and assist in water retention, while also providing a surface for sensory perception.

Internally, African fat-tailed geckos have a simple but efficient organ system. Their heart is three-chambered, consisting of two atria and one ventricle, which allows for some separation of oxygenated and deoxygenated blood but is less efficient than the four-chambered hearts of mammals. Their lungs are relatively simple sacs that function efficiently when provided with appropriate oxygen levels, temperature, and humidity.

The eyes of African fat-tailed geckos are adapted for nocturnal activity, with large pupils that allow them to detect subtle movement in low-light conditions. Unlike many reptiles, they lack eyelids and instead have a transparent spectacle covering the eye, which they clean with their tongue. Understanding these anatomical traits helps owners appreciate the gecko's behavior and design enclosures that accommodate their sensory and physical needs.

Shedding, Growth, and Weight Management

Shedding, or ecdysis, is a natural process in which reptiles periodically shed their outer layer of skin to accommodate growth, remove parasites, and maintain skin health. In African fat-tailed geckos, shedding occurs more frequently during juvenile stages when growth rates are rapid and becomes less frequent as the gecko reaches maturity. Shedding can last several days, and it is important for owners to provide appropriate humidity levels and rough surfaces to help the gecko remove old skin. Retained shed, particularly on toes or the tail, can cause circulation problems and must be addressed promptly.

Growth and weight management are equally crucial for maintaining long-term health. Juvenile geckos experience rapid growth during the first year, which gradually slows as they approach adulthood. Owners should monitor weight regularly to detect underfeeding, overfeeding, or health issues. A healthy African fat-tailed gecko maintains a plump tail, smooth skin, and consistent body condition, with neither excessive thinness nor obesity.

Nutrition, temperature, and overall husbandry directly affect growth rates. Overfeeding or feeding inappropriate food items can lead to obesity, while underfeeding or poor nutrition may result in stunted growth or weakened immune function. Understanding these dynamics allows keepers to adjust feeding schedules and portion sizes to promote optimal development.

How Temperature, Humidity, and Light Affect Metabolism and Behavior

Environmental conditions are fundamental to reptile biology because African fat-tailed geckos rely on external cues to regulate metabolism. Temperature influences digestion, immune function, activity levels, and reproductive cycles. Fat-tailed geckos require a thermal gradient within their enclosure, typically with a warm side between 88–92°F (31–33°C) and a cooler side around 75–80°F (24–27°C). This allows the gecko to self-regulate body temperature by moving between areas.

Humidity is equally important. While African fat-tailed geckos are adapted to semi-arid environments, low humidity can lead to shedding problems, dehydration, and respiratory issues. Providing a controlled humidity level of approximately 40–60%, along with a humid hide during shedding, helps maintain hydration and supports skin health. Conversely, excessively high humidity can encourage fungal or bacterial growth, so proper ventilation is necessary.

Light also plays a role, though African fat-tailed geckos are nocturnal. While they do not rely heavily on UVB radiation like some diurnal reptiles, low-level UVB exposure can support vitamin D synthesis, calcium metabolism, and general health. Additionally, a consistent day-night cycle reinforces circadian rhythms, influencing feeding, activity, and rest patterns.

Digestive and Excretory Systems: Understanding Feeding and Waste

The digestive system of African fat-tailed geckos is relatively simple but highly specialized for insectivorous diets. Food passes from the mouth to the esophagus and then to a simple stomach where enzymes and gastric acids break down nutrients. The small intestine absorbs these nutrients efficiently, while waste moves into the large intestine and cloaca for excretion. This system is optimized for high-protein diets, and feeding inappropriate foods can lead to impaction, nutrient deficiencies, or other digestive issues.

Excretion occurs via the cloaca, which expels both fecal matter and urates (a semi-solid form of nitrogenous waste common in reptiles). Observing the appearance, consistency, and frequency of waste is an important diagnostic tool for health monitoring. Normal feces are firm, segmented, and dark in color, while urates are typically white or cream-colored and pasty. Abnormalities, such as diarrhea, discolored feces, or prolonged absence of waste, can indicate dietary issues, dehydration, or underlying illness.

Proper digestion and waste elimination are directly influenced by environmental conditions, nutrition, and overall health. By understanding the digestive and excretory systems, owners can make informed decisions about feeding schedules, portion sizes, and hydration, ensuring that their geckos thrive in captivity.

In conclusion, understanding the biology of African fat-tailed geckos provides the foundation for effective husbandry. Knowledge of anatomy, growth patterns, shedding, temperature regulation, humidity needs, and digestive processes equips keepers to create a healthy environment, monitor well-being, and respond to potential problems. This biological insight is not only essential for maintaining health but also enhances the keeper's ability to observe, appreciate, and interact with their gecko in a way that respects its natural behaviors and long-term welfare.

Three

Chapter 3: Preparing for Your Gecko

Bringing an African fat-tailed gecko into your home is an exciting step, but preparation is essential for the health and well-being of the animal. Unlike more conventional pets, reptiles require specialized care and a carefully controlled environment. Proper planning ensures that your gecko can thrive, reduces stress for both owner and pet, and sets the stage for a long, healthy life. This chapter covers key considerations, including assessing readiness for reptile ownership, choosing between captive-bred and wild-caught geckos, selecting the right equipment, and maintaining safety and hygiene.

Determining Readiness for Reptile Ownership

Before acquiring an African fat-tailed gecko, it is important to evaluate your ability to meet its long-term needs. These geckos have an average lifespan of 15 to 20 years in captivity, meaning ownership is a long-term commitment. Prospective keepers should consider whether they have the time, financial resources, and living environment to provide consistent care over decades. Unlike dogs or cats, reptiles cannot express discomfort or illness vocally, so owners must be observant and proactive in monitoring health and behavior.

Time commitment includes daily feeding, weekly habitat maintenance, and seasonal adjustments in temperature and humidity. Owners should also be prepared for occasional veterinary care, which may involve specialized reptile veterinarians. Financial readiness is equally critical, as quality equipment, live food, supplements, and vet visits contribute to ongoing expenses. Finally, potential keepers should evaluate household factors, such as other pets, children, or roommates, to ensure the gecko's safety and minimize stress.

Choosing Between Captive-Bred vs. Wild-Caught Geckos

A key decision in acquiring a gecko is whether to choose a captive-bred or wild-caught individual. Captive-bred African fat-tailed geckos are highly recommended for beginners and ethical keepers. These geckos are typically healthier, more accustomed to human interaction, and less stressed by captivity. Captive breeding programs also help reduce pressure on wild populations and support sustainable pet keeping.

Wild-caught geckos, in contrast, may carry parasites, diseases, or nutritional deficiencies and are often more skittish. They may require a longer acclimation period and more intensive care to adjust to captive conditions. Additionally, removing geckos from the wild can contribute to population decline and environmental disruption. When possible, choose a reputable breeder or pet store that prioritizes health, ethics, and proper husbandry practices. Ask about the gecko's age, diet, and any medical history before making a purchase.

Necessary Equipment: Terrarium Size, Substrate, Hides, Heating, and Lighting

Creating a suitable habitat is one of the most important aspects of preparation. African fat-tailed geckos are terrestrial, so horizontal space within the enclosure is more critical than height. A single adult typically thrives in a 20-gallon terrarium, while juveniles can start in smaller enclosures with the option to upgrade as they grow. The tank should allow for distinct thermal zones to facilitate thermoregulation.

Substrate choices vary, but they should balance comfort, hygiene, and safety. Reptile carpet, paper towels, or tile are safe and easy to clean options. Loose substrates, such as sand or soil, can be used cautiously, but must be monitored to prevent ingestion, which can cause impaction. Providing multiple hides is essential, including a warm hide on the heated side of the enclosure, a cooler hide, and a humid hide to assist with shedding. Hides offer security, reduce stress, and mimic the gecko's natural environment.

Heating is critical because African fat-tailed geckos are ectothermic. A reliable heat source, such as an under-tank heating pad or ceramic heat emitter, creates a temperature gradient from warm (88–92°F / 31–33°C) to cool (75–80°F / 24–27°C). Thermometers placed at both ends of the tank help monitor conditions accurately. Lighting should simulate a natural day-night cycle. While fat-tailed geckos are nocturnal and do not require intense UVB, low-level UVB lighting can be beneficial for overall health, including vitamin D synthesis and calcium metabolism.

Safety and Hygiene Considerations

Safety and hygiene are fundamental for both the gecko and the keeper. Enclosures should be secure, with tight-fitting lids or screens to prevent escapes. Electrical cords for heat sources must be managed to avoid burns or accidents, and all equipment should be designed for reptile use to prevent toxic exposures. Sharp objects or overly rough surfaces should be avoided to prevent injury.

Hygiene practices are critical to prevent the spread of bacteria, fungi, and parasites. Hands should always be washed before and after handling the gecko, especially since reptiles can carry Salmonella. Food and water dishes should be cleaned and sanitized regularly, and uneaten live prey should be removed promptly to avoid contamination. Substrate and hides require regular cleaning and replacement, and waste should be disposed of in a manner that minimizes exposure to pathogens.

Additionally, the habitat should be inspected daily for hazards, such as broken decorations, damp spots, or mold growth. Maintaining a clean and safe environment not only prevents illness but also encourages natural behaviors, reduces stress, and enhances the overall well-being of the gecko.

Preparation is a critical first step in responsible African fat-tailed gecko ownership. By carefully assessing readiness, choosing a captive-bred gecko, acquiring appropriate equipment, and establishing robust safety and hygiene practices, owners lay the foundation for a healthy and thriving pet. Thoughtful preparation ensures that both the keeper and the gecko enjoy a rewarding and long-term relationship. Taking the time to understand these essential elements before bringing a gecko home is an investment that pays off in the animal's health, behavior, and longevity.

Four

Chapter 4: Setting Up the Ideal Habitat

Creating an appropriate habitat is one of the most crucial steps in ensuring the health and well-being of an African fat-tailed gecko. Unlike some pets that can adapt easily to a wide range of environments, geckos rely entirely on their enclosure to provide proper temperature, humidity, hiding places, and stimulation. A well-planned habitat not only supports their physiological needs but also encourages natural behaviors, reduces stress, and contributes to longevity. This chapter explores how to design an ideal enclosure, select substrates, manage temperature and humidity, and incorporate enriching elements for both beginners and experienced keepers.

Creating a Proper Enclosure Layout

African fat-tailed geckos are terrestrial, meaning they spend most of their time on the ground rather than climbing. Therefore, horizontal space is far more important than vertical height. A standard adult gecko thrives in a 20-gallon terrarium, though larger enclosures can offer additional enrichment and space for exercise. Juveniles may begin in smaller tanks but should be moved to larger setups as they grow to accommodate increasing size and activity levels.

When arranging the enclosure, it is essential to create distinct thermal zones. One side should provide warmth for digestion and activity, while the other should remain cooler to allow thermoregulation. Hides, water dishes, and decor should be positioned strategically to balance accessibility with security. Avoid cluttering the tank excessively, as geckos require open space to move freely and explore. A well-organized layout also simplifies cleaning and monitoring.

Substrate Options and Their Pros and Cons

Selecting an appropriate substrate is critical for hygiene, comfort, and safety. Several options are commonly used in African fat-tailed gecko enclosures:

- **Paper Towels**: Simple, inexpensive, and easy to replace. Ideal for beginners or quarantine setups but offers minimal enrichment.
- **Reptile Carpet**: Reusable and safe, providing a solid surface without ingestion risks. Requires regular cleaning and occasional replacement.
- **Tile or Slate**: Durable, easy to clean, and mimics natural rocky surfaces. Offers excellent thermal conduction for heat pads but may feel hard underfoot.
- **Loose Substrates (Sand, Soil, Coconut Fiber)**: Can encourage burrowing behavior and create a more naturalistic environment. Must be monitored closely, as ingestion can cause impaction, particularly in juveniles.

Choosing a substrate depends on the keeper's priorities—ease of maintenance, aesthetics, enrichment, or naturalism. Many keepers combine multiple substrates to create zones for hiding, basking, and burrowing.

Temperature Gradients and Basking Areas

Temperature regulation is a cornerstone of reptile husbandry. African fat-tailed geckos require a thermal gradient, allowing them to self-regulate their body temperature. The warm side of the tank should range between 88–92°F (31–33°C), while the cooler side can remain around 75–80°F (24–27°C). Under-tank heating pads are often preferred because they provide localized warmth and encourage natural belly-basking behavior.

A basking area should be included on the warm side of the enclosure.

While fat-tailed geckos are nocturnal and do not require intense basking, access to a warm area aids digestion, metabolic function, and overall vitality. Thermometers should be placed on both sides of the tank to monitor the gradient, and owners should check temperatures regularly to ensure consistency. Heating devices should be regulated with a thermostat to prevent overheating and reduce the risk of burns.

Humidity Management: Why It Matters and How to Maintain It

Although African fat-tailed geckos are adapted to semi-arid environments, proper humidity is essential for skin health and successful shedding. A humidity range of approximately 40–60% is ideal for everyday maintenance, while higher localized humidity in a humid hide assists during shedding.

Humidity can be maintained using several methods:

- **Humid Hides**: Small containers or boxes filled with damp moss, paper towels, or coconut fiber provide a controlled humid environment for shedding. The gecko can enter voluntarily to maintain hydration.
- **Misting**: Light, occasional misting helps maintain ambient humidity, but excessive spraying can create damp areas that promote fungal growth.
- **Substrate Choice**: Some substrates, such as coconut fiber or soil, naturally retain moisture, aiding humidity control. However, they must be monitored to avoid mold.

Proper humidity management not only supports shedding but also reduces stress, prevents respiratory issues, and promotes overall health. Regular monitoring with a hygrometer ensures that conditions remain within safe limits.

Decorating for Enrichment: Hides, Climbing Structures, and Tactile Elements

Environmental enrichment is essential for encouraging natural behaviors and preventing boredom. African fat-tailed geckos benefit from a combination of hiding spots, climbing opportunities, and tactile surfaces that simulate their natural habitat. Key considerations include:

- **Hides**: Provide at least two to three hides in different areas, including a warm hide, a cool hide, and a humid hide. Hides give geckos security, reduce stress, and encourage exploration.
- **Climbing Structures**: Although primarily terrestrial, geckos may occasionally climb low rocks or branches. Low, stable climbing elements can add variety without increasing the risk of falls or injury.
- **Tactile Elements**: Substrate textures, small rocks, or flat platforms allow geckos to engage in natural behaviors such as digging, scratching, and exploring. Variation in surfaces also contributes to mental stimulation and physical activity.

Decor should be arranged to balance accessibility and safety. Avoid sharp edges or unstable structures, as geckos can injure themselves when startled or climbing. A thoughtfully decorated habitat mimics natural conditions, supports thermoregulation, and creates a visually appealing environment for the keeper.

Setting up the ideal habitat for an African fat-tailed gecko involves more than simply providing a tank. A well-planned enclosure considers horizontal space, thermal gradients, humidity, substrate, and enrichment to meet both physiological and behavioral needs. By carefully selecting materials, arranging hides, and monitoring environmental conditions, keepers create a safe, stimulating, and healthy environment that supports natural behaviors and long-term well-being. Proper habitat setup is the foundation of successful gecko ownership, ensuring that these fascinating reptiles can thrive and exhibit their unique behaviors in captivity.

Five

Chapter 5: Feeding and Nutrition Essentials

Proper nutrition is a cornerstone of African fat-tailed gecko care. A well-balanced diet not only supports growth and overall health but also impacts behavior, energy levels, and longevity. Understanding what these geckos eat in the wild, how to replicate those nutritional needs in captivity, and how to monitor their intake ensures that your pet remains healthy throughout its life. This chapter covers natural and captive diets, feeding techniques, supplements, feeding frequency, and recognizing signs of nutritional deficiencies.

Natural Diet Versus Captive Diet Considerations

In the wild, African fat-tailed geckos are opportunistic insectivores. They consume a variety of insects and small invertebrates, including crickets, beetles, roaches, and moths. Occasional consumption of other small arthropods or insect larvae provides additional nutritional diversity. Wild geckos rely on live prey that moves, which stimulates hunting behavior, contributes to mental stimulation, and encourages natural energy expenditure.

Replicating this diet in captivity requires careful planning. While captive geckos can thrive on commercially available insects, offering a variety of prey items is important to prevent nutritional gaps and encourage natural foraging behaviors. It is also essential to consider the nutritional quality of captive prey. Many store-bought insects may be low in key nutrients such as calcium and vitamin D3, which are critical for skeletal health and metabolic function.

Feeding Live Insects and Commercially Available Foods

Live insects are the primary food source for captive African fat-tailed geckos. Common options include crickets, mealworms, superworms, roaches, and silkworms. These insects should be appropriately sized—generally no larger than the space between the gecko's eyes—to prevent choking or impaction. Feeding multiple prey types ensures balanced nutrition and helps prevent dietary monotony.

Commercially available gecko diets, including formulated insectivore powders or pellets, can supplement or occasionally replace live insects. These products are designed to provide a complete nutritional profile but should not entirely replace live prey unless specifically formulated for long-term maintenance. Many keepers use a combination approach, offering live insects for stimulation and enrichment while supplementing with fortified powders to ensure adequate nutrition.

Gut-loading is a critical step when feeding live prey. This process involves feeding insects nutrient-rich foods—such as leafy greens, grains, or specialized gut-loading formulas—24 to 48 hours before offering them to the gecko. Gut-loading enhances the nutritional content of the prey and ensures that geckos receive adequate vitamins, minerals, and calories with every meal.

Nutritional Supplements: Calcium, Vitamins, and Gut-Loading

Calcium and vitamin supplementation are essential for preventing metabolic bone disease and other deficiencies in African fat-tailed geckos. A dusting of calcium powder, applied to live insects prior to feeding, helps maintain strong bones and proper growth, particularly in juveniles. Some keepers alternate calcium with or without added vitamin D3, depending on the presence and intensity of UVB exposure in the enclosure.

Multivitamin powders can be used periodically to support overall health. However, over-supplementation can be harmful, so it is important to follow recommended dosages and adjust based on the gecko's exposure to natural or artificial UVB. Combining gut-loading, calcium supplementation, and periodic multivitamins ensures that captive diets approximate the nutritional quality of a wild diet.

Feeding Frequency and Monitoring Appetite

Feeding frequency varies with age and size. Juvenile geckos generally require daily feeding to support rapid growth, while adults can be fed every other day or three times per week depending on appetite and activity levels. The amount of food offered should encourage consumption within a short period, typically 15–30 minutes, with any uneaten insects removed promptly to prevent spoilage or stress to the gecko.

Monitoring appetite is an important indicator of health. A consistent appetite suggests that husbandry conditions, temperature, and diet are appropriate, while reduced feeding may signal stress, illness, or improper environmental conditions. Observing feeding behavior also provides insight into individual preferences, allowing keepers to adjust the types and quantities of prey offered.

Identifying Signs of Nutritional Deficiencies

Recognizing early signs of nutritional deficiencies is critical to prevent long-term health problems. Common indicators include:

- **Weakness or lethargy**: May indicate insufficient caloric intake or mineral imbalances.
- **Soft or pliable bones, tail, or jaw**: Early signs of calcium deficiency or metabolic bone disease.
- **Poor growth or stunted development in juveniles**: Can result from inadequate feeding frequency or nutrient-poor diets.
- **Abnormal shedding**: Often associated with dehydration or vitamin/mineral deficiencies.
- **Loss of appetite or weight loss**: Can indicate systemic health issues or imbalanced nutrition.

Early detection and intervention—adjusting diet, supplements, and environmental conditions—can prevent severe illness and improve overall health outcomes. Routine observation, weight monitoring, and consistent feeding practices form the foundation for maintaining optimal nutrition and long-term well-being.

Feeding and nutrition are central to the health and happiness of African fat-tailed geckos. By understanding their natural diet, providing a varied and nutritionally complete captive diet, using appropriate supplementation, and monitoring feeding behavior, keepers can ensure that their geckos thrive. Proper attention to dietary needs not only supports growth, energy, and longevity but also reinforces natural behaviors such as hunting, exploration, and interaction with the environment. With careful planning and observation, feeding becomes both a practical care routine and an enriching, rewarding aspect of gecko ownership.

Chapter 6: Understanding Behavior and Handling

Understanding the behavior of African fat-tailed geckos is essential for fostering a healthy and trusting relationship with your pet. Observing body language, respecting individual temperaments, and learning safe handling techniques can significantly reduce stress and prevent injury. This chapter explores typical behavior patterns, social interaction, handling best practices, and recognizing signs of stress, fear, and aggression.

Typical Behavior Patterns and Body Language

African fat-tailed geckos are primarily nocturnal and terrestrial, spending most of the day hiding and emerging at night to hunt or explore. They are generally calm and deliberate in their movements, reflecting a cautious approach to new environments. Their activity levels can fluctuate with temperature, humidity, and time of day, and they may display bursts of energy during feeding or exploration.

Body language is a key indicator of a gecko's mood and comfort level. Common postures include:

- **Relaxed posture**: Limbs tucked comfortably under the body, tail slightly curved or resting naturally, and smooth skin. This indicates a calm, content gecko.
- **Alert posture**: Eyes wide open, head raised, and body slightly elevated. The gecko is attentive to its surroundings, often when investigating new objects or noises.
- **Defensive posture**: Body flattened, tail curled over the back, or tail tapping. This may precede an attempt to flee or signal discomfort with handling or environmental changes.

Observing these cues helps keepers anticipate reactions and interact appropriately.

Social Interaction: Tolerances and Individual Differences

African fat-tailed geckos are generally solitary animals and do not require social interaction with other geckos. While they can coexist with others under specific circumstances—such as in large enclosures or controlled breeding environments—keeping multiple geckos together increases the risk of territorial disputes, stress, or injury. It is important to monitor individual behavior and intervene if aggression or persistent stress occurs.

Individual differences are pronounced in this species. Some geckos are naturally more tolerant of handling and exploration, while others are shy or easily stressed. Recognizing and respecting these personality traits allows keepers to tailor interactions, reduce fear responses, and build trust over time. Patience and consistent routines often yield greater confidence and willingness to interact.

Safe and Stress-Free Handling Techniques

Handling African fat-tailed geckos requires care to prevent injury and minimize stress. Key techniques include:

- **Approach calmly**: Move slowly and avoid sudden movements or loud noises. Allow the gecko to see your hand before attempting contact.
- **Support the body**: Always support the gecko's entire body, including the limbs and tail. Avoid pinching or restraining the tail, as it is a vital fat

storage organ and can be dropped if threatened.
- **Use minimal restraint**: Allow the gecko to move freely over your hand or arm. Restrictive handling increases stress and may lead to defensive behaviors.
- **Limit handling time**: Short, gentle interactions are preferable, especially for new or shy geckos. Gradually increase duration as the gecko becomes more comfortable.

Consistency and gentleness help the gecko associate handling with safety rather than threat, promoting trust and reducing stress-related behaviors.

Recognizing Stress, Fear, and Aggression Signals

Identifying stress, fear, and aggression is crucial to prevent injury and maintain health. Common signs include:

- **Tail wagging or lashing**: A warning signal indicating irritation or potential defensive action.
- **Hissing or clicking sounds**: Rare but may occur when the gecko feels threatened.
- **Flattened body or crouching**: Indicates fear or readiness to flee.
- **Attempting to escape or bite**: Aggressive behaviors are usually defensive rather than predatory.
- **Loss of appetite or prolonged hiding**: Chronic stress can affect feeding behavior and overall health.

Environmental factors such as incorrect temperature, high noise levels, or inappropriate handling often contribute to stress. Addressing these conditions promptly can restore comfort and well-being. Providing ample hides, a secure enclosure, and gradual acclimation to human interaction helps reduce anxiety and fosters positive behaviors.

Understanding behavior and handling is fundamental to responsible African fat-tailed gecko care. Recognizing typical behaviors, respecting individual temperaments, using safe handling techniques, and identifying stress or aggression signals allows keepers to build a trusting, healthy relationship with their pet. Observing and responding to these behavioral cues not only enhances interaction but also supports long-term physical and psychological health. By combining careful observation with gentle, consistent handling, owners create an environment where their gecko feels secure, stimulated, and confident, setting the stage for a rewarding lifelong companionship.

Seven

Chapter 7: Health Monitoring and Common Illnesses

Maintaining the health of an African fat-tailed gecko requires consistent observation, knowledge of common ailments, and proactive care. Unlike mammals or birds, reptiles cannot verbally indicate discomfort or illness, so the responsibility rests entirely on the keeper to recognize subtle signs of distress. Understanding the hallmarks of a healthy gecko, identifying early symptoms of disease, and knowing when to seek veterinary assistance are essential components of responsible ownership.

Signs of a Healthy Gecko

A healthy African fat-tailed gecko exhibits several distinct physical and behavioral characteristics. Observing these signs regularly helps keepers distinguish between normal variations and potential health concerns. Key indicators include:

- **Clear, bright eyes**: Eyes should be free of discharge or cloudiness, reflecting good hydration and eye health.
- **Smooth, intact skin**: Healthy skin appears uniform in color and texture

without lesions, discoloration, or retained shed.
- **Plump tail**: A thick, well-rounded tail indicates proper fat storage and overall nutritional health.
- **Normal movement**: The gecko moves fluidly and purposefully, showing coordinated limb function and alertness.
- **Consistent appetite**: Regular feeding behavior and eagerness to hunt live prey demonstrate good digestive and metabolic function.
- **Regular shedding**: Occasional, complete shedding with no retained skin suggests proper hydration and humidity levels.

Behavioral signs also indicate wellness. A gecko that explores its environment, uses hides appropriately, and reacts to stimuli with calm curiosity is typically in good health.

Recognizing Early Signs of Disease

Early detection of illness is vital for effective treatment. African fat-tailed geckos are susceptible to several common health problems, including respiratory infections, parasites, and skin issues. Recognizing subtle symptoms can prevent conditions from progressing to life-threatening stages.

- **Respiratory infections**: Often caused by poor ventilation, excessive humidity, or low temperatures. Symptoms include wheezing, gaping mouth, labored breathing, nasal discharge, and lethargy. Early intervention with a veterinarian is crucial to prevent deterioration.
- **Parasites**: Internal parasites, such as nematodes or protozoans, can lead to weight loss, diarrhea, and irregular feces. External parasites like mites may cause skin irritation, excessive scratching, and restlessness. Fecal examinations and professional treatment are necessary for diagnosis and management.
- **Skin issues**: Retained shed, fungal infections, or wounds can result from inadequate humidity, substrate problems, or enclosure hazards. Signs include crusty or discolored patches, persistent scratching, or areas of missing scales. Addressing environmental causes and seeking veterinary guidance ensures proper healing.

Chapter 7: Health Monitoring and Common Illnesses

Routine observation, including daily visual checks and weekly physical inspections, allows keepers to detect these early warning signs before they escalate.

Common Injuries and Their Treatment

Even in carefully maintained enclosures, African fat-tailed geckos may sustain injuries that require attention. Common injuries include tail damage, cuts or abrasions from sharp objects, and broken toes or limbs. Treatment depends on the severity:

- **Tail injuries**: If the tail is partially damaged, clean the area with a reptile-safe antiseptic and monitor for infection. Minor injuries usually heal, but severe trauma may require veterinary evaluation. Remember that geckos can drop their tail voluntarily when threatened, and a regenerated tail may differ in appearance.
- **Cuts and abrasions**: Minor wounds should be cleaned gently and kept dry. Monitor for swelling, redness, or discharge, which may indicate infection.
- **Broken limbs or toes**: Any suspected fracture requires veterinary assessment. Immobilization, environmental modification, and professional care are often necessary to ensure proper healing and prevent permanent deformity.

Preventing injuries through careful enclosure setup, safe decorations, and appropriate handling is the most effective strategy. Avoid overcrowding enclosures, remove sharp edges, and supervise interactions with other geckos when applicable.

The Importance of Regular Vet Check-Ups and Finding a Reptile Vet

While routine observation is critical, professional veterinary care is equally important. Regular check-ups with a veterinarian experienced in reptiles provide preventive care, early diagnosis, and treatment of health issues. Vets can perform fecal exams, blood tests, and physical assessments to ensure optimal health.

Finding a qualified reptile veterinarian may require research, as not all general practice vets are equipped to treat exotic species. Look for clinics or specialists with experience in lizards, preferably with positive reviews from other reptile keepers. Establishing a relationship with a reptile vet before emergencies arise ensures that prompt, knowledgeable care is available when needed.

Emergency situations, such as severe respiratory distress, persistent lethargy, or sudden injury, require immediate attention. Keepers should be prepared with contact information, transport protocols, and a safe container for travel to minimize stress on the gecko.

Health monitoring is a cornerstone of responsible African fat-tailed gecko ownership. By recognizing the signs of a healthy gecko, detecting early symptoms of disease, understanding common injuries, and maintaining access to qualified veterinary care, keepers can ensure their pets live long, vibrant lives. Observant and proactive care not only prevents serious health problems but also fosters a deeper understanding of the gecko's needs, behavior, and well-being. Through consistent attention and timely intervention, owners provide an environment in which their African fat-tailed geckos can thrive physically, mentally, and emotionally.

Eight

Chapter 8: Shedding, Growth, and Molting Care

Shedding, growth, and molting are natural and ongoing processes in the life of an African fat-tailed gecko. Understanding these processes is critical for providing appropriate care and ensuring the gecko's long-term health. Improper management of shedding or failure to monitor growth can lead to serious health problems, including retained skin, infections, and developmental issues. This chapter explores the shedding cycle, strategies for supportive care, handling retained shed, and monitoring growth and development over time.

Understanding the Shedding Cycle and Its Significance

Shedding, or ecdysis, is the process by which reptiles periodically remove their outer layer of skin to allow for growth, remove parasites, and maintain skin health. In African fat-tailed geckos, shedding occurs more frequently in juveniles due to rapid growth and becomes less frequent in adults. A typical shedding cycle may last from a few days to a week, during which the skin becomes dull, opaque, and often whitish or grayish in appearance.

Shedding serves several vital functions:

- **Facilitates growth**: As geckos grow, their skin must expand to accommodate a larger body size.
- **Removes parasites and dead skin**: Shedding helps eliminate external parasites and maintains healthy skin.
- **Indicates health and hydration**: Regular, complete sheds reflect proper nutrition, hydration, and husbandry, while incomplete or irregular shedding may signal underlying issues.

Recognizing the stages of shedding allows keepers to provide targeted support and reduces stress during this vulnerable period.

Proper Care During Shedding: Humidity, Hydration, and Observation

Shedding is a sensitive time, and proper care can prevent complications. The most critical factors are humidity, hydration, and observation:

- **Humidity**: African fat-tailed geckos are adapted to semi-arid conditions but require higher localized humidity during shedding. Providing a humid hide—such as a container with damp sphagnum moss or paper towels—creates an environment that softens the skin and facilitates easy removal. Ambient humidity should remain moderate, around 40–60%, while the humid hide provides a concentrated area of moisture.
- **Hydration**: Adequate hydration is essential for healthy shedding. Ensure a fresh water source is available at all times. Some keepers lightly mist the humid hide to maintain moisture levels, but avoid soaking the enclosure, which can encourage fungal growth.
- **Observation**: Monitor the gecko during the shedding process. Check for areas of retained skin, particularly around the toes, tail tip, and eyes, where shedding complications are most common. Gentle observation helps detect problems early, allowing for timely intervention.

Maintaining a stable environment during shedding minimizes stress and promotes a smooth, complete cycle.

Dealing with Retained Shed or Stuck Toes

Chapter 8: Shedding, Growth, and Molting Care

Retained shed, especially around toes and tail tips, is a common issue that can lead to tissue damage, infections, or loss of digits if left untreated. Intervention requires care:

- **Soaking**: Place the gecko in a shallow, lukewarm water bath for 10–15 minutes to soften the retained skin. Ensure the water level is shallow enough to prevent drowning and that the gecko can remain upright.
- **Gentle removal**: Use a soft cloth, damp cotton swab, or your fingers to carefully peel away loose skin. Avoid pulling forcefully, as this can cause injury.
- **Humid environment**: After treatment, return the gecko to a humid hide for several hours to ensure complete shedding and hydration.

Persistent retained skin or repeated shedding issues may indicate inadequate humidity, poor nutrition, or underlying health problems. Consultation with a reptile veterinarian is recommended if complications persist.

Monitoring Growth and Development Over Time

Regular monitoring of growth and development is crucial, particularly in juveniles. Weight and length measurements provide objective data to ensure the gecko is thriving:

- **Weight tracking**: Use a digital scale to measure weight weekly. Steady, incremental growth indicates proper nutrition and care, while sudden weight loss or stunted growth may signal health concerns.
- **Visual assessment**: Observe body condition, tail thickness, and muscle tone. A plump tail and well-rounded body indicate adequate fat stores and good nutrition.
- **Shedding frequency**: Younger geckos shed more often, while adults shed less frequently. Deviations from expected patterns may suggest environmental or dietary issues.
- **Behavioral cues**: Active, alert geckos with a normal appetite are likely growing appropriately. Lethargy, hiding excessively, or disinterest in food may indicate stress or illness affecting growth.

Documenting growth trends over time enables keepers to make informed adjustments to diet, enclosure conditions, and care routines, ensuring optimal development and longevity.

Shedding, growth, and molting are fundamental aspects of African fat-tailed gecko biology. By understanding the shedding cycle, providing appropriate humidity and hydration, managing retained skin carefully, and monitoring growth, keepers can prevent complications and promote healthy development. Consistent observation and proactive intervention not only maintain physical health but also strengthen the bond between gecko and keeper. Proper care during these natural processes lays the foundation for a long, healthy, and rewarding relationship with your African fat-tailed gecko.

Nine

Chapter 9: Breeding Basics and Genetics

Breeding African fat-tailed geckos is a complex yet rewarding aspect of reptile keeping. Successful breeding requires a thorough understanding of sex determination, sexual maturity, mating behaviors, egg care, and the genetic principles that influence color and pattern variations. This chapter provides an in-depth guide for keepers interested in ethical and responsible breeding practices while emphasizing animal welfare and proper husbandry.

Identifying Males and Females

Sex determination is the first step in breeding. African fat-tailed geckos exhibit distinct physical differences between males and females, although juveniles may be more challenging to sex accurately. Key distinguishing features include:

- **Hemipenal bulges**: Males possess noticeable bulges at the base of the tail, just behind the vent. These bulges house the hemipenes, which are used during copulation.
- **Preanal pores**: Males display a row of small, prominent preanal pores along the underside near the vent, which secrete pheromones. These pores are generally absent or less pronounced in females.

- **Body size and shape**: Females tend to have slightly wider bodies, particularly around the abdomen, to accommodate egg development, while males may appear more streamlined.

Accurate sexing is essential to avoid aggression or breeding mistakes. Handling should be gentle, and if there is uncertainty, consultation with an experienced breeder or veterinarian can provide confirmation.

Understanding Sexual Maturity and Breeding Readiness

Sexual maturity in African fat-tailed geckos depends on age, size, and overall health. Typically, males reach maturity around 10–12 months, while females mature slightly later at 12–18 months. Size is a more reliable indicator than age alone; females should weigh at least 45–50 grams to ensure they can safely produce and lay eggs without compromising health.

Before initiating breeding, both geckos must be in optimal condition. Adequate fat reserves in the tail, consistent appetite, and regular shedding cycles indicate readiness. Geckos that are underweight, stressed, or frequently ill should not be bred, as this can endanger their health and the viability of offspring.

Mating Behavior, Incubation, and Egg Care

Breeding behaviors are typically subtle but observable. During courtship, males may exhibit:

- **Tail twitching**: A rapid, rhythmic movement used to attract the female's attention.
- **Gentle nudging**: The male may use his snout or body to encourage interaction.
- **Chasing or following**: A sign of interest in the female's readiness for copulation.

Females may display receptivity by remaining calm and allowing the male to engage without aggressive resistance. Aggressive behavior from either gecko indicates incompatibility or stress, and breeding attempts should be paused.

After successful mating, females will develop eggs over a 4–6 week period.

Typically, a clutch contains one to two eggs, although larger clutches are possible in older or healthier females. Egg-laying requires a suitable nesting area with slightly moistened substrate to maintain proper humidity. Ideal incubation conditions involve consistent temperatures between 82–88°F (28–31°C) and moderate humidity, which support embryo development and successful hatching.

Monitoring eggs for signs of mold, desiccation, or collapse is essential. Incubators or dedicated hatching containers provide controlled conditions, improving hatching success rates. Eggs generally hatch within 50–60 days, depending on temperature and humidity.

Genetics and Morphs: Understanding Color and Pattern Variations

Genetics play a central role in the appearance of African fat-tailed geckos. Captive breeding has produced a variety of morphs, including albino, high yellow, patternless, and blizzard variants. Understanding inheritance patterns, dominant and recessive traits, and selective pairing allows breeders to predict offspring appearances responsibly.

- **Dominant traits**: These require only one copy of the gene to be expressed in the phenotype. Examples include certain high yellow or patternless traits.
- **Recessive traits**: Both parents must carry the gene for the trait to appear in offspring. Many albino or specific pattern morphs follow this inheritance pattern.
- **Co-dominant and polygenic traits**: Some morphs are influenced by multiple genes, producing a range of variations in coloration, banding, and pattern intensity.

Responsible breeding involves careful record-keeping, ethical selection of breeding pairs, and prioritizing the health and welfare of the geckos over aesthetic traits. Avoid inbreeding or pairing geckos that are too closely related, as this can result in health complications and reduced genetic diversity.

Breeding African fat-tailed geckos requires knowledge, preparation, and ethical responsibility. By accurately identifying sexes, understanding sexual maturity, observing mating behaviors, providing proper incubation care, and applying genetic principles responsibly, keepers can achieve successful and healthy reproduction. Emphasizing the welfare of both parents and offspring ensures that breeding remains a positive, enriching aspect of gecko ownership. Understanding genetics and morph variations also adds an educational dimension, allowing keepers to appreciate the complexity of inheritance while maintaining sustainable and ethical breeding practices.

Ten

Chapter 10: Advanced Feeding and Dietary Enrichment

Feeding African fat-tailed geckos goes beyond basic nutrition; advanced dietary practices can enhance physical health, mental stimulation, and natural behaviors. Providing a variety of prey, incorporating enrichment techniques, adjusting diets seasonally, and maintaining long-term digestive health are essential for keeping geckos active, engaged, and thriving. This chapter explores strategies for advanced feeding that support both physiological and behavioral well-being.

Introducing Live Prey Variety and Enrichment Techniques

While crickets and mealworms form the staple diet of most captive African fat-tailed geckos, introducing a variety of prey items can provide additional nutrients and prevent dietary monotony. Suitable options include:

- **Roaches**: Dubia roaches are highly nutritious, easy to breed, and provide a different texture and movement pattern compared to crickets.
- **Silkworms**: Soft-bodied and easy to digest, silkworms are rich in protein and low in fat.
- **Hornworms and Waxworms**: Ideal as occasional treats due to higher

fat content. Overfeeding these can lead to obesity, so moderation is key.

Enrichment techniques involve presenting prey in ways that stimulate hunting behavior. Hiding insects under leaves, inside cork tubes, or using live prey that actively moves encourages natural stalking and pouncing behaviors. This mental and physical stimulation promotes exercise, reduces boredom, and enhances overall well-being.

Feeding Challenging Prey for Stimulation

Occasionally offering more challenging prey items can simulate natural foraging and improve hunting skills. For example:

- **Larger crickets or roaches**: Slightly larger prey encourages geckos to exercise patience, stalking, and pouncing techniques.
- **Prey in enclosures with obstacles**: Placing insects in areas that require climbing over rocks or navigating small obstacles promotes exploration and problem-solving.

While challenging prey should be offered sparingly to prevent frustration or stress, these exercises enrich the gecko's environment and foster natural behaviors that may otherwise be limited in captivity. Observing hunting strategies during these sessions provides insight into individual personalities and abilities.

Seasonal Adjustments in Diet and Feeding Behavior

In the wild, African fat-tailed geckos experience seasonal fluctuations in prey availability, which affect feeding behavior and metabolism. Captive keepers can mimic these patterns to maintain natural rhythms and support long-term health:

- **Winter or cooler months**: Geckos may naturally reduce feeding activity. Offering smaller, less frequent meals while maintaining temperature and humidity prevents overfeeding during periods of lower activity.
- **Spring and summer**: Increased activity levels and growth spurts require more frequent feeding and higher-quality prey to support metabolic

demands.
- **Breeding season**: Females may require additional nutrition and calcium supplementation to support egg production, while males may exhibit heightened activity and feeding responses.

Adjusting diet seasonally maintains a balance between caloric intake and energy expenditure, preventing obesity or malnutrition and promoting natural physiological cycles.

Maintaining Digestive Health in Long-Term Captivity

Long-term digestive health depends on consistent feeding practices, high-quality prey, and attention to environmental conditions. Key considerations include:

- **Prey preparation**: Gut-loading insects 24–48 hours before feeding ensures adequate nutrient content. Dusting prey with calcium and vitamin supplements supports bone health and overall nutrition.
- **Observation of waste**: Regularly monitoring feces and urates provides insight into digestive efficiency and overall health. Changes in color, consistency, or frequency may indicate dietary imbalances or health issues.
- **Avoiding overfeeding**: Excessive prey can lead to obesity, slowed metabolism, and fatty deposits in the liver. Maintaining appropriate portion sizes supports long-term vitality.
- **Hydration**: Adequate water availability facilitates digestion and prevents impaction. Incorporating hydrated prey items or occasional misting of prey can further aid digestive function.

Providing consistent, varied, and nutritionally complete feeding ensures that African fat-tailed geckos maintain optimal digestion, energy levels, and long-term health.

Advanced feeding practices enhance both the physical and behavioral health of African fat-tailed geckos. By introducing a variety of live prey, incorporating enrichment and challenging feeding techniques, adjusting diets seasonally, and maintaining digestive health, keepers support natural behaviors and long-term well-being. These strategies transform feeding from a routine task into an opportunity for stimulation, learning, and observation, fostering a richer and more engaging environment. Consistent attention to diet and enrichment ensures that geckos remain active, alert, and healthy throughout their lives, highlighting the importance of advanced care for long-term captive success.

Eleven

Chapter 11: Creating a Long-Term Care Plan

Owning an African fat-tailed gecko is a long-term commitment that requires careful planning, consistent monitoring, and a proactive approach to husbandry. These geckos can live 15 to 20 years or more in captivity, and their health and quality of life depend heavily on attentive care over decades. Developing a comprehensive long-term care plan helps keepers maintain proper nutrition, environmental conditions, and financial readiness, ensuring that both the gecko and the keeper enjoy a sustainable, rewarding relationship.

Record-Keeping: Feeding, Weight, Shedding, and Health Logs

Maintaining detailed records is one of the most effective tools for long-term gecko care. Documenting feeding schedules, weight, shedding cycles, and health observations allows keepers to detect patterns, identify early warning signs, and make informed adjustments.

- **Feeding logs**: Record the type and quantity of prey offered, frequency of feeding, and consumption. Noting preferences or refusals helps track appetite changes and potential health concerns.
- **Weight tracking**: Weighing geckos regularly—weekly or biweekly—provides objective insight into growth, fat storage, and overall condition.

Sudden weight loss or gain can indicate illness or nutritional imbalances.
- **Shedding records**: Document the timing, duration, and completeness of sheds. Irregular or incomplete shedding may point to humidity or hydration issues.
- **Health notes**: Record observations regarding activity, behavior, and any signs of stress, injury, or illness. Tracking veterinary visits, treatments, and outcomes ensures continuity of care over the years.

Keeping a physical notebook, digital spreadsheet, or specialized reptile care app can simplify long-term monitoring and create a valuable reference for troubleshooting future health or husbandry challenges.

Planning for Decades-Long Ownership

African fat-tailed geckos are long-lived, and responsible ownership requires anticipating the challenges of decades-long care. Planning includes:

- **Housing longevity**: Enclosures, heating elements, and lighting should be selected for durability and ease of maintenance over many years. Upgrading or replacing worn components periodically prevents habitat deterioration.
- **Continuity of care**: Life events such as relocation, job changes, or family circumstances can impact care. Establish backup caretakers or contingency plans to ensure uninterrupted attention.
- **Health monitoring over time**: Regular veterinary check-ups, parasite prevention, and environmental adjustments are critical to maintain vitality in both juvenile and adult geckos.

Long-term planning emphasizes sustainability, ensuring that the gecko's environment, nutrition, and care remain consistent and high-quality throughout its lifespan.

Seasonal Care Adjustments: Temperature, Lighting, and Activity Levels

Geckos experience natural variations in activity and metabolism based on seasonal cues, which should be reflected in their care. Seasonal adjustments help mimic natural conditions and maintain optimal health:

- **Temperature**: Slightly lower ambient temperatures during cooler months can encourage natural metabolic fluctuations, while maintaining safe ranges. During warmer months, ensure that the enclosure does not exceed ideal heat levels.
- **Lighting**: Adjusting day-night cycles to reflect seasonal changes supports natural rhythms, influencing activity, feeding, and overall behavior. Even though African fat-tailed geckos are nocturnal, subtle variations in photoperiod can enhance well-being.
- **Activity levels**: Geckos may reduce activity during cooler periods. Observing these patterns and adjusting feeding frequency and prey size accordingly prevents overfeeding and supports healthy metabolism.

By aligning environmental conditions with seasonal changes, keepers create a dynamic habitat that promotes natural behaviors and long-term health.

Budgeting for Long-Term Expenses

Financial planning is an essential component of responsible ownership. Long-term care involves recurring and occasional costs, including:

- **Food and supplements**: Regular purchase of live insects, gut-loading materials, and vitamin/calcium powders.
- **Habitat maintenance**: Replacement or upgrading of substrates, hides, heating pads, thermostats, and lighting.
- **Veterinary care**: Routine check-ups, emergency visits, and specialized treatments.
- **Unexpected costs**: Addressing illnesses, injuries, or environmental failures requires a financial cushion

Estimating annual expenses and setting aside funds for emergencies ensures that the gecko's care remains uninterrupted, regardless of unforeseen circumstances. A long-term budget helps maintain consistency in husbandry, which is critical for health and longevity.

Creating a long-term care plan is vital for sustaining the health and well-being of an African fat-tailed gecko over its 15–20 year lifespan. Through meticulous record-keeping, planning for decades-long ownership, adjusting care seasonally, and budgeting for ongoing expenses, keepers can provide a stable, enriched environment that meets all physiological and behavioral needs. A well-structured long-term plan not only enhances the gecko's life but also offers peace of mind for the keeper, ensuring that this rewarding companionship can flourish for decades.

Twelve

Chapter 12: Problem-Solving and Troubleshooting

Even with careful planning and attentive care, African fat-tailed geckos can encounter behavioral or health challenges. Effective problem-solving involves identifying the underlying causes, adjusting husbandry practices, and knowing when to seek professional veterinary care. This chapter provides a comprehensive guide to addressing common behavioral issues, appetite and weight concerns, environmental problems, and decision-making regarding veterinary intervention.

Common Behavioral Issues: Aggression, Hiding, and Stress Behaviors

Behavioral problems often signal underlying stress, environmental discomfort, or health issues. Recognizing these patterns is the first step in resolution:

- **Aggression**: Although typically docile, geckos may become defensive when stressed, handled improperly, or housed with incompatible individuals. Aggressive behaviors include biting, tail lashing, or repeated attempts to escape. Solutions involve reviewing handling techniques, providing adequate hides, and ensuring solitary housing for adult geckos to reduce territorial conflicts.

- **Excessive hiding**: Spending prolonged periods in hides may indicate fear, discomfort, or illness. Evaluate temperature, lighting, and substrate for suitability, and observe feeding patterns to ensure the gecko is eating normally. Gradual, calm handling and enrichment can encourage more active exploration.
- **Stress behaviors**: Tail twitching, repeated pacing, gaping mouth, or refusal to feed are signs of stress. Environmental stability, proper temperature gradients, and secure hides can alleviate stress, while sudden changes in enclosure setup should be minimized.

Behavioral issues often resolve with consistent, patient adjustments to husbandry and environmental enrichment.

Appetite Loss and Weight Concerns

A sudden or prolonged change in appetite or weight is a common indicator of health or environmental problems:

- **Causes**: Appetite loss may result from stress, illness, improper temperatures, poor humidity, or recent shedding. Weight loss can also indicate parasite infestations, metabolic issues, or dietary deficiencies.
- **Monitoring**: Track feeding behavior and weight regularly. Weigh geckos weekly to detect gradual changes and maintain detailed logs for reference.
- **Intervention**: Address environmental factors first, ensuring proper temperature gradients, humidity, and food quality. Offer a variety of live prey to stimulate interest. If appetite loss persists beyond a few days, or if weight loss is significant, veterinary consultation is warranted.

Timely observation and intervention prevent minor issues from developing into serious health concerns.

Environmental Problems: Humidity, Temperature, and Substrate Issues

Environmental conditions are a primary contributor to both behavioral and health problems. Maintaining consistent, species-appropriate conditions is crucial:

- **Humidity issues**: Low humidity can lead to incomplete shedding, dry skin, and stress, while excessive humidity can promote fungal infections and respiratory problems. Use hygrometers and humid hides to maintain balance.
- **Temperature problems**: Incorrect gradients affect metabolism, digestion, and activity levels. A too-cool enclosure may cause lethargy and appetite loss, while excessive heat can lead to dehydration and stress. Thermometers and thermostats ensure reliable monitoring and control.
- **Substrate concerns**: Ingestible or inappropriate substrates (e.g., sand for juveniles) can cause impaction. Damp or moldy substrates increase the risk of skin infections. Choosing safe, easy-to-clean substrates supports both health and behavior.

Regular environmental audits, along with careful monitoring of gecko behavior and health, prevent problems before they escalate.

When to Consult a Vet Versus Adjusting Husbandry

Distinguishing between issues that can be resolved through husbandry adjustments and those requiring veterinary intervention is essential:

- **Adjusting husbandry**: Minor behavioral changes, occasional shedding difficulties, or brief appetite fluctuations may be managed by optimizing temperature, humidity, substrate, hides, and enrichment. Observing responses over several days provides insight into effectiveness.
- **Veterinary consultation**: Persistent appetite loss, weight loss, visible injury, abnormal feces, respiratory symptoms, or chronic behavioral changes require professional evaluation. Reptile veterinarians can diagnose and treat underlying conditions that are not apparent through observation alone.

Maintaining a relationship with a qualified reptile vet ensures that timely medical care is available when needed, reducing risk of serious illness or injury.

Problem-solving and troubleshooting are integral to responsible African fat-tailed gecko ownership. By recognizing common behavioral issues, monitoring appetite and weight, addressing environmental problems, and knowing when to consult a veterinarian, keepers can maintain optimal health and well-being for their geckos. Effective observation, careful adjustment of husbandry, and timely professional intervention prevent minor concerns from becoming serious, supporting long-term, stress-free care. With vigilance, patience, and knowledge, keepers can confidently navigate challenges, ensuring their geckos thrive in captivity.

Chapter 13: Enrichment, Exercise, and Mental Stimulation

African fat-tailed geckos benefit from more than just the basic necessities of food, water, and shelter. Mental and physical stimulation are critical for maintaining their overall health, reducing stress, and encouraging natural behaviors. Enrichment helps prevent lethargy, supports healthy metabolism, and promotes problem-solving abilities. This chapter explores strategies for creating an engaging environment, providing safe opportunities for exercise, establishing enrichment routines, and understanding the impact of mental stimulation on well-being.

Designing an Engaging and Dynamic Environment

A dynamic enclosure mimics aspects of a gecko's natural habitat, providing both physical and sensory stimulation. Key elements include:

- **Varied terrain**: Use rocks, branches, and textured surfaces to create a range of climbing and exploration opportunities. Even primarily terrestrial geckos enjoy navigating over or around objects.
- **Hides and shelters**: Multiple hides at different temperature and humidity zones offer security and encourage movement between areas,

supporting natural thermoregulation.
- **Visual stimuli**: Naturalistic backgrounds, contrasting textures, and non-toxic plants create interest and curiosity without overwhelming the gecko.
- **Changing layouts**: Occasionally rearranging elements promotes exploration and prevents habituation, though changes should be gradual to avoid stress.

A thoughtfully designed environment encourages natural behaviors such as climbing, stalking, and exploring, enhancing both physical and mental health.

Safe Climbing, Exploration, and Hiding Opportunities

While African fat-tailed geckos are not arboreal, providing safe climbing opportunities can encourage exercise and enrichment:

- **Low, stable climbing structures**: Use branches, cork tubes, or rock formations that are secure and appropriately sized to prevent falls or injury.
- **Tactile diversity**: Incorporate surfaces with varying textures, such as smooth rocks, cork bark, or moss pads, to stimulate tactile exploration.
- **Accessible hides**: Offer multiple hiding spots, including a humid hide for shedding and dry hides for day-time rest. The ability to choose where to retreat promotes comfort and reduces stress.

Exercise and exploration encourage natural behaviors, maintain muscle tone, and prevent obesity. Safe, well-designed features allow geckos to exercise without risk of injury or excessive stress.

Enrichment Routines for Indoor Geckos

Regular enrichment routines provide both mental and physical stimulation, which is especially important for geckos confined to indoor enclosures. Effective strategies include:

- **Targeted feeding challenges**: Hide live prey or use shallow containers that require problem-solving to access food, promoting hunting behav-

iors.
- **Scent exploration**: Introduce new scents using safe, non-toxic materials to stimulate olfactory senses.
- **Environmental rotation**: Periodically rearranging décor or introducing novel objects encourages curiosity and exploration.
- **Observation periods**: Gentle interaction and quiet observation allow the gecko to engage with the keeper while remaining in control, enhancing trust and mental stimulation.

Consistency in enrichment routines fosters predictable stimulation while maintaining a sense of safety, balancing novelty with security.

Understanding How Mental Stimulation Impacts Health

Mental stimulation is closely linked to physical health. Geckos that are under-stimulated may exhibit stress behaviors, reduced appetite, and lethargy, which can negatively impact immune function and overall well-being. Conversely, enriched environments:

- **Promote exercise**: Encouraging movement prevents obesity, strengthens muscles, and supports digestion.
- **Enhance natural behaviors**: Hunting, climbing, and exploring reinforce instincts and cognitive function.
- **Reduce stress**: Engaged geckos display lower stress levels, which contributes to longer lifespan and improved shedding cycles.
- **Support learning and adaptation**: Exposure to varied environments helps geckos adjust to minor changes and develop confidence, reducing fear responses.

By integrating mental stimulation into daily care, keepers support holistic well-being, creating a more active, alert, and healthy gecko.

Enrichment, exercise, and mental stimulation are vital components of African fat-tailed gecko care. A dynamic, engaging environment, safe climbing and hiding opportunities, structured enrichment routines, and recognition of the benefits of mental stimulation all contribute to improved physical health, reduced stress, and enhanced quality of life. Providing these elements transforms the gecko's enclosure into a vibrant, stimulating habitat, fostering natural behaviors and ensuring long-term wellness. Through thoughtful enrichment and careful observation, keepers can cultivate a more rewarding and interactive relationship with their gecko.

Fourteen

Chapter 14: Ethical Considerations and Community Engagement

Owning an African fat-tailed gecko carries ethical responsibilities that extend beyond individual care. Responsible keepers consider the welfare of their gecko, the impact of their choices on wild populations, and the broader reptile-keeping community. Engagement with like-minded enthusiasts, educational outreach, and ethical decision-making are essential components of long-term, responsible ownership. This chapter explores ethical responsibilities, sustainable sourcing, rehoming practices, and community involvement.

Ethical Responsibilities of Keeping Exotic Pets

Keeping exotic pets like African fat-tailed geckos requires a commitment to meeting their physiological, psychological, and social needs throughout their lifespan. Ethical responsibilities include:

- **Providing proper care**: Ensuring appropriate diet, habitat, lighting, temperature, and enrichment to maintain health and well-being.
- **Commitment to long-term care**: Recognizing that geckos can live 15–20 years, requiring consistent attention, record-keeping, and adapta-

tion to age-related needs.
- **Avoiding neglect or abandonment**: Responsible owners must plan for changes in personal circumstances to prevent geckos from being neglected or released into unsuitable environments.
- **Promoting welfare over aesthetics**: When selecting morphs or breeding for color variations, prioritize health and temperament over appearance.

Ethical ownership emphasizes a proactive, informed approach that prioritizes the gecko's welfare and long-term quality of life.

Avoiding Wild-Caught Geckos and Supporting Captive Breeding

The exotic pet trade has significant implications for wild populations. Wild-caught African fat-tailed geckos face habitat destruction, capture stress, and mortality during transport. Responsible keepers support conservation and sustainability by:

- **Choosing captive-bred geckos**: Captive-bred geckos are typically healthier, better adapted to captivity, and contribute less to the depletion of wild populations.
- **Verifying breeder practices**: Ensure that breeders prioritize animal welfare, genetic diversity, and responsible breeding techniques.
- **Educating others**: Promote awareness of the environmental and ethical consequences of wild-caught geckos, encouraging responsible sourcing within the community.

Supporting captive breeding programs helps preserve natural populations while maintaining a sustainable pet trade that aligns with ethical practices.

Rehoming and Adoption Best Practices

Circumstances may arise where a gecko must be rehomed. Ethical practices for rehoming include:

- **Careful vetting of adopters**: Ensure that potential new owners understand the species' needs, lifespan, and commitment requirements.

- **Avoiding impulsive sales or giveaways**: Geckos should never be released into the wild, as this can disrupt ecosystems and threaten the gecko's survival.
- **Providing support and education**: Share detailed care instructions, health history, and enclosure specifications to ensure continuity of proper care.
- **Engaging with rescue networks**: Reputable reptile rescue organizations can assist with finding responsible homes and provide guidance on ethical adoption practices.

Responsible rehoming maintains the gecko's welfare while supporting a community-oriented approach to exotic pet ownership.

Engaging with Herpetology Communities, Forums, and Social Groups

Community engagement enriches knowledge, supports ethical practices, and fosters lifelong learning. Opportunities include:

- **Online forums and discussion groups**: Platforms such as herpetology forums, social media groups, and reptile-focused communities allow keepers to share experiences, troubleshoot issues, and exchange best practices.
- **Local clubs and herpetology societies**: Joining clubs provides access to workshops, events, and mentorship opportunities, promoting responsible care and networking with experienced keepers.
- **Educational outreach**: Sharing accurate information about gecko care, breeding ethics, and conservation contributes to public awareness and helps prevent misinformation in the broader community.
- **Participation in conservation initiatives**: Supporting captive breeding programs, rescue efforts, and habitat protection projects strengthens the ethical foundation of pet keeping.

Engagement with the wider community fosters responsible stewardship, collaboration, and advocacy, enhancing both the gecko's welfare and the credibility of the hobby.

Ethical considerations and community engagement are essential pillars of responsible African fat-tailed gecko ownership. By prioritizing the welfare of their geckos, supporting captive breeding, practicing responsible rehoming, and actively participating in herpetology communities, keepers can positively impact both individual animals and the broader reptile-keeping ecosystem. Ethical ownership goes beyond daily husbandry; it encompasses sustainability, education, and collaboration, ensuring that the hobby promotes conservation, well-being, and lifelong learning.

Fifteen

Chapter 15: Lifelong Learning and Conservation Awareness

Owning an African fat-tailed gecko is a journey that extends beyond daily care. Responsible keepers commit to lifelong learning, ongoing adaptation of husbandry practices, and active participation in conservation and education. Understanding the latest research, supporting ethical trade, mentoring new keepers, and preparing for aging geckos ensures both the gecko's welfare and the keeper's ongoing development. This chapter explores strategies for continued education, conservation involvement, mentorship, and adapting care over the lifespan.

Staying Updated with Research, Husbandry Techniques, and Morphs

The field of reptile husbandry is continually evolving, with new research providing insights into behavior, nutrition, breeding, and disease prevention. Staying informed allows keepers to provide optimal care:

- **Scientific literature**: Peer-reviewed journals and studies provide credible information about physiology, genetics, and environmental requirements.
- **Husbandry guides and books**: Updated guides on African fat-tailed

geckos offer practical advice on enclosure setup, diet, and enrichment strategies.
- **Morph research**: Knowledge of emerging morphs and their genetic implications enables responsible breeding and helps avoid health issues linked to inbreeding or undesirable traits.
- **Online forums and webinars**: Engaging with reputable online communities and attending workshops provides access to practical experience, troubleshooting advice, and current best practices.

Continuous education ensures that care routines evolve alongside scientific and community knowledge, enhancing the gecko's quality of life.

Supporting Conservation Efforts and Responsible Trade

African fat-tailed geckos, like many reptiles, are affected by habitat loss and the exotic pet trade. Keepers play a vital role in promoting conservation and ethical trade:

- **Promoting captive-bred geckos**: Encouraging and sourcing only captive-bred animals reduces pressure on wild populations.
- **Participating in conservation programs**: Supporting organizations involved in habitat protection, breeding programs, or educational outreach contributes to species preservation.
- **Advocating for ethical trade**: Educating others about the ecological consequences of wild capture helps cultivate responsible behavior within the community.

Active involvement reinforces the ethical framework of reptile keeping and ensures that the hobby supports sustainability and species protection.

Becoming a Mentor for New Keepers

Experienced keepers have the opportunity to guide newcomers, promoting responsible practices and sharing knowledge gained over years of hands-on experience:

- **Providing practical guidance**: Advising on enclosure setup, diet,

enrichment, and health monitoring helps beginners avoid common pitfalls.
- **Encouraging ethical practices**: Mentors can emphasize the importance of captive breeding, long-term commitment, and proper handling, fostering a culture of responsibility.
- **Sharing troubleshooting strategies**: Offering insight on behavioral issues, illness prevention, and environmental management equips new keepers with practical tools for success.
- **Creating community connections**: Introducing novices to clubs, online forums, and local reptile groups strengthens the network of informed, conscientious keepers.

Mentorship contributes to the longevity of responsible practices in the hobby and ensures the welfare of countless geckos across the community.

Embracing Lifelong Care: Preparing for Aging Geckos and Adapting Routines

As African fat-tailed geckos age, their needs change, requiring adjustments to care routines:

- **Monitoring health changes**: Older geckos may experience reduced mobility, slower metabolism, or dental issues. Regular observation, veterinary check-ups, and record-keeping help detect subtle health changes early.
- **Adjusting diet and feeding schedules**: Aging geckos may require smaller prey, softer foods, or more frequent supplementation to maintain nutrition and fat stores.
- **Modifying habitat**: Lower climbing structures, additional hides, and stable temperature gradients accommodate reduced agility and comfort needs.
- **Maintaining mental stimulation**: Continuing enrichment activities tailored to mobility and sensory changes prevents boredom and stress in older geckos.

By anticipating age-related changes and adapting husbandry practices accordingly, keepers ensure that their geckos enjoy comfort, health, and quality of life throughout their lifespan.

Lifelong learning and conservation awareness are integral to responsible African fat-tailed gecko ownership. Staying informed about research and husbandry practices, supporting ethical trade, mentoring new keepers, and preparing for aging geckos all contribute to sustainable and rewarding care. Commitment to continuous education and ethical stewardship not only enhances the gecko's welfare but also strengthens the broader community of reptile enthusiasts. By embracing lifelong care, keepers cultivate a deeper connection with their pets while promoting conservation, education, and responsible practices that endure across generations.

Printed in Dunstable, United Kingdom